THE SUSSEX OUSE

GW00370484

by

Terry Owen

(who found the Way)

and

Peter Anderson

(who found the words)

"The stream invites us to follow: the impulse is so common that it might be set down as instinct; and certainly there is no more fascinating pastime than to keep company with a river from its source to the sea."

A H Hudson, *Afoot in England* 1903

Other titles by the authors – A Companion on the South Downs Way
The Tandridge Border Path
An Ashdown Forest Perambulation
West Sussex Literary Trail (Peter Anderson)
I Spy What and Why on the South Downs Way
Abingworth – a Brief History (Terry Owen)

Per-Rambulations came into being in response to the Millennium when it created the Tandridge Border Path with the sponsorship of Tandridge District Council and the support of Surrey County Council. Between them the members have designed and led walks both voluntarily and professionally throughout the south east of England and also lead walks for HF Holidays.

Per-Rambulations looks for ways that go beyond mere mileage. It hopes to point the way to Kipling's six honest serving-men: What and Why: When and How: Where and Who. Above all there must always be time and place "to stand and stare".

Whilst the authors have walked and researched the entire route for the purposes of this guide, no responsibility can be accepted for any unforeseen circumstances encountered while following it.

The publishers would, however, greatly appreciate any information regarding material changes, and any problems encountered.

First published in 2005 by Per-Rambulations
Second edition published in 2012
Designed by *IntegrityDesignandPrint@hotmail.co.uk*

All photographs and content © Per-Rambulations except front cover Tom Bailey

Per-Rambulations

www.per-rambulations.co.uk

Contents

For ease of reference, route directions are shown in coloured panels.

The maps in this book are for illustrative purposes only.

Walkers are strongly recommended to rely on the relevant Ordnance Survey maps.

The Sussex Ouse Valley Way exists through the collaboration of the East and West Sussex County Councils, what was in 2005 the Sussex Downs Conservation Board and the authors.

It started as a concept in the minds of the authors. After establishing the route they took the concept to the County Councils and the Conservation Board who embraced it. It was brought to fruition in the synergy that was created between all the parties.

Follow the Countryside Code

- Be safe – plan ahead and follow any signs

- Leave gates and property as you find them

- Protect plants and animals, and take your litter home

- Keep dogs under close control

- Consider other people

Foreword

Walking in the wilderness can bring us into the closest tune with nature.

A mainly quiet river valley in south east England may seem far removed from the wilderness that it once was when an almost unbroken band of woodland stretched between the North and South Downs and man needed his survival skills to exist there. But you do not have to be somewhere half a world away that is exotic or difficult to reach to achieve a closer relationship with nature. An ideal place may be only a short journey away or even on the doorstep.

It was not far away from that river valley that, on the North Downs, I began to learn my own bushcraft skills, becoming an ardent student of nature and learning to treat her with respect, which she returns with kindness. In spite of many travels since, Britain remains my favourite place and a walk in the woodlands of Sussex can be an ideal introduction to country lore.

The Sussex Ouse Valley Way has been planned as more than the pleasant walk through quintessentially English countryside that it is. It is a journey; it may be on a small scale but it tells a story too of how and why things have become as they are. As with many a walk, it is like stepping onto the pages of a history book. The Way is steeped in history not always most noticeable: beside the looming presence of Lewes Castle, but not obvious, there is the site of the battle that may have laid the foundations of parliamentary democracy. And all along the way there are signs of the lives and works of those long passed.

It is hoped that those who follow the Way will look with open eyes and understanding and wonder as they pass through the rich diversity of landscape and animal and plant life and that curiosity and the wish to discover more are awakened.

Ray Mears, Bushcraft Expert, TV Presenter and Author

The Sussex Ouse Valley Way

Lower Beeding to Staplefield Common	7 miles / 11 km
Staplefield Common to Lindfield	7½ miles / 12 km
Lindfield to Newick	7 miles / 11 km
Newick to Barcombe Mills	6 miles / 9.5 km
Barcombe Mills to Rodmell	8 miles / 13 km
Rodmell to Seaford Bay	6½ miles / 10.5 km
Lower Beeding to Seaford Bay	**42 miles / 67 km**

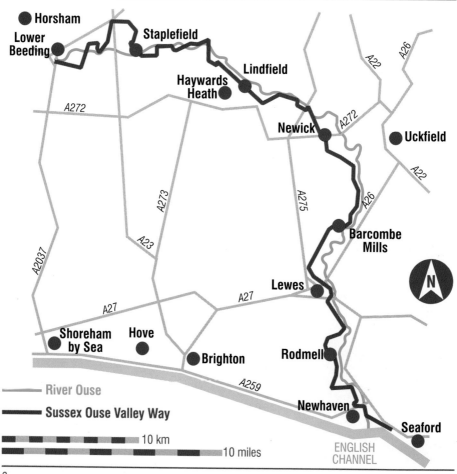

Introduction

"There is some holiness in the rising of rivers, and a great attachment to their springs."

Hilaire Belloc, *The Four Men*

The Way lies inside the valley of the Sussex Ouse but is not confined to the river. That might be wanted but it is not possible. There is no public right of way of any form that runs the length of the river and, sometimes, where there is a stretch of public path that runs alongside the river, that has been omitted due to the impossibility of linking it with viable pathways open to the public without using busy open roads.

The counties of East and West Sussex fall within five main landscape characteristic areas and provide an incredible diversity of scenery within a comparatively small compass. Those five areas are the High Weald, the Low Weald, the South Downs, the Wealden Greensand and the Coastal Plain. The Way starts in the High Weald, crosses into the Low Weald and passes through the South Downs south of Lewes.

In very simple terms, the Weald is the area of land between the North and South Downs, partly in Sussex but also taking in parts of Surrey and Kent. As with many places in Sussex, once the kingdom of the South Saxons, the Saxons were responsible for the name. To them it was Andredesweald, the great area of thick woodland that lay beyond the Roman port of Anderida, now known as Pevensey: woodland that was up to 120 miles long and 40 miles wide. Both the High Weald and the Low Weald remain comparatively well wooded but only to a fraction of the extent of that described by Bede (c673-725 AD) as *"thick, and inaccessible, the abode of deer, swine and wolves"*.

There are no simple definitions that would make the High Weald and the Low Weald instantly recognisable and easily distinguishable. Indeed, there is much internal diversity within their own separate areas. In comparative terms again, the High Weald is higher than the Low Weald but it does not reach any mathematically commanding heights. Nowhere is it above 240 metres AOD (Above Ordnance Datum) although the sweeping views from the heathland of Ashdown Forest, which itself contrasts with much of the remainder of the High Weald, give an opposite impression.

Characteristic of the High Weald are wooded ridges cut deeply by steep sided stream valleys, or ghylls, examples of which can be seen along the Way at Leonardslee and at Nymans. The Low Weald which surrounds the High Weald on three sides to the north, west and south, is more gently undulating with a patchwork of fields and small woodlands. There can be no mistaking the broad sweep of the South Downs when the Way reaches them.

The Sussex Ouse, the southernmost of the three English Rivers Ouse, is, however, central to the Ouse Valley. It is wholly a Sussex river. It rises in West Sussex and flows into the sea over 30 miles later at Newhaven in East Sussex. The end is clear but the start is not.

One suggested source is the water that gushes to flow south from Furnace Pond that lies a kilometre to the west of the village of Slaugham (pronounced Slaffham). Some have put it at a "*grotto*" beneath a bridge where the waters flow from the mill pond close by Slaugham Place. And, although both these two points may have a force of water bursting forth to give the impression of a river impatient to be off, the truth, like the source of the Thames, may be more

prosaic. Both Furnace Pond and the mill pond are themselves fed by streams, the mill pond from the west by a flow lying on private ground but already called the Ouse on the largest scale Ordnance Survey maps.

Perhaps it is safest to leave the matter with William Camden, the Elizabethan antiquarian and historian. After mentioning Brighthelmsted, now better known to us as Brighton, he wrote in his Britannia, first published in 1586:

"*A few miles hence a nameless river falls into the sea from the forest of St Leonard near Slaugham the residence of the Coverts who were knights here t. Henry III.*"

The Ouse cascading from Slaugham Mill Pond

We shall meet the Coverts on the journey but Camden indicates another area of uncertainty: the origin of the name. Although the word, Ouse, as with the other Rivers Ouse, can be derived from an ancient origin indicating a use before the Norman Conquest of 1066, this would not appear to be the case with the Sussex Ouse. As is shown by the quotation from Camden, the Sussex river does not appear to have been known as the Ouse until sometime after the late 16th century. The river was certainly known from the 13th century, at least in its upper and middle reaches, as Midewinde or middle winding, possibly because in the days when Sussex was a single entity, the river was in the middle dividing Sussex in two. The name of the river was preserved in the name of the Midwyn (pronounced Midwine) Bridge near Lindfield where the B2028 crosses the river now known as Lindfield Bridge and marked as such on the Ordnance Survey map.

There are theories why the river became known as the Ouse. One is that the expression *agua de Lewes* (water of Lewes), recorded in the 13th century, was wrongly copied as *agua del Ewes*, Ewes to become corrupted to Ouse, but in reality, nobody knows.

But, wherever the river starts, and whatever it is called, it now flows, in the main, peacefully through rural countryside from start to finish, passing through only one town at Lewes until it reaches the sea at Newhaven. Its greatest disturbances now are caused by acts of nature, especially the flooding that has happened more than once in its long history. The devastation caused in the year 2000 was not unique although, perhaps, aggravated by intervening human activities. The river is accepted as a natural part of the scenery. There is, however, very little, if any, English scenery that is entirely natural, untouched by the hand of man. When man no longer uses, nature has no hesitation in stepping back in again although not always as wanted.

So it is with the Sussex Ouse. It has played and still plays a role in the affairs of men . It was literally one of the driving forces when the South East was a centre of heavy industry and has been a transport artery reaching into the heart of Sussex. The Ouse, together with Ardingly Reservoir, is still a significant supply source of public water. But when we follow the valley of the Sussex Ouse, we take a pathway that on the surface passes in the main through a seemingly quiet, rural countryside; a path, however, that covers much of the history of man's development.

Lower Beeding to Staplefield Common

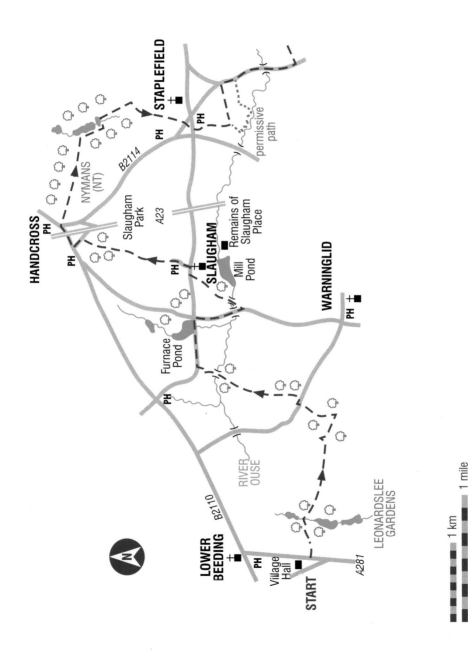

Lower Beeding to Staplefield Common

Distance – 7 miles / 11 km

Map – OS Explorer 134: Crawley & Horsham

"Out of the Weald, the secret Weald,
Men sent in ancient years
The horse-shoes red at Flodden-Field,
The arrows at Poitiers!"

Rudyard Kipling, *Puck's Song*

The route starts by meandering through mixed but typical High Wealden scenery: fields, woodland and water including one of the large and beautiful ponds that once served the iron industry.

Walking today through the valley of the Sussex Ouse thoughts are far from heavy industry and yet the Weald, in which the northerly parts of the valley lie, was once the industrial heartland of England – the *"black country"* of its day.

More than two thousand years ago the Celtic Iron Age people, whose hill forts and burial mounds still dominate heights throughout the South Downs, produced iron in the Weald, an activity that the Romans when they arrived, in the words of one authority, *"set about exploiting with considerable vigour"*. Local production of iron slowed to a trickle after the Romans departed, reviving again in the Middle Ages to become a major heavy industry in the 16th, 17th and 18th centuries, its best known product being cannon – that, in the best traditions of the armaments industry, were supplied to all sides, including the enemy.

The Weald held the three necessary ingredients.

First, iron ore, for although iron is the fourth most widely distributed element on earth, it only occurs in a usable form in a limited number of places of which the Weald is one.

Secondly, wood to provide charcoal for the fuel to smelt (heat) the ore in a furnace and to produce carbon that is essential to the process of making iron.

Thirdly, water that drove the mill when the process became more mechanised.

The small furnace in the early days, where the draught was provided by hand operated bellows, is known as a *bloomery* and the iron produced is *wrought iron* that had to be hammered (or wrought) both to remove impurities and to achieve the required shape. Later water power was harnessed to drive the furnace and hammer mills that received their water supplies from Furnace and Hammer Ponds. The mills provided the draught to the larger furnaces by bellows too big to be operated by human hands and the iron was wrought in the hammer mills by great trip hammers.

The major development came with the blast furnace that was introduced into England in 1496, the first being at Newbridge on Ashdown Forest. This enabled much higher temperatures to be achieved. That, in turn, meant that molten iron could be cast into moulds rather than lumps being beaten into shape, although in the early days the moulded lumps of iron were then beaten instead of being moulded into final forms.

The list of surviving iron products from the Weald makes somewhat curious and limited reading: cannon and cannon balls: andirons (firedogs) and firebacks: monumental slabs that can still be seen in churches in Sussex and, in 1710, the railings at Wren's St. Paul's Cathedral in the City of London. But the more mundane items get lost to view or, being iron, disintegrate.

Slaugham Mill Pond

Amongst other things there are references from the 13th and 14th centuries to nails, horseshoes, arrows and rims for wagon wheels and there were, no doubt, many other items of everyday use although the majority of the iron produced in the Weald was taken elsewhere as iron bars to be turned unto finished objects.

When the molten cast iron was tapped from the furnaces, it ran in a series of channels to a larger mould and it was said that the comb shape produced was like a female pig suckling her piglets. It was called a *pig*: hence the term *pig iron*: to be technically correct the lump of iron produced was a *sow* if the casting was over 1,000 pounds (453 kilos): a *pig* if under that weight.

Although there are now few survivors, cannon played a huge part in the later development of the Sussex iron industry. As the use of artillery grew, pressure mounted for alternative supplies. The best guns of the time were made of bronze, had to be bought abroad and were expensive. Home produced iron guns provided a viable and cheaper alternative.

The barrels of early iron guns were made in separate lengths and had to be banded together just like a wooden barrel. In 1543 the first iron gun to be cast in one piece in England is said to have been produced by Ralph Hogge of Buxted, not far from Uckfield. The bore of the cannon, the business part where the cannon balls go, was literally bored out with a huge drill giving rise to another expression in common use. Cannon balls had probably been cast from an earlier date making redundant the masons who had followed armies chipping out replacement ammunition or gunstones from stone.

The end of the iron industry in Sussex came with the final closing of the last remaining works at Ashburnham although the industry had been declining for many years previously. As in modern times, economics were the reason: iron could be produced more efficiently and cheaply elsewhere: not abroad, but from the growing heavy industries in the north of England and Scotland.

The allegation is often made that it was the iron masters who denuded the countryside of woodland. That was not so. Agriculture was primarily responsible for such clearances. The iron masters needed woodland to provide a renewable source of coppiced underwood to make charcoal and not the large timber that is unsuitable for that purpose: and so, the woods with names such as *Hammer Wood*. The Way passes through one of these just behind the Sloop Inn at Freshfield Bridge.

This area of the Weald is now quiet but, in the 16th century, William Camden wrote of the hammers, *"whose incessant noise day and night echoes all over the neighbourhood".*

> Leave **Lower Beeding** Village Hall car park, turn right. After 100m cross road to enter driveway.

Lower Beeding where the Way begins is, as Hilaire Belloc pointed out in his book *The Four Men,* one of those contradictory, not to say contrary, Sussex names. Lower Beeding is inland and on high whilst Upper Beeding… *"is at the very lowest part in the whole County of Sussex"*. According to Belloc this was part of Adam's plan when naming all the places on earth to distinguish the paradise that is Sussex from everywhere else, and to give… *"names of a sort that should give fools to think"*. This also produces… *"the square place called Roundabout"*. *"Or the Broadbridge, which is so narrow* (or was when Belloc was writing) *that two carts cannot pass on it"*.

> At gateway to *Keepers Cottage*, turn right onto wide track and descend into woods. Bear right and right again by fingerposts over water courses and then ascend left on narrow path into woods. Path reaches high wire fence.

On the other side of the fence lie the 240 acre gardens of Leonardslee. Described by E V Lucas in 1904 as, *"one of the most satisfying estates in the county"*, the gardens were started in 1801 when Charles Beauclerk, using hammer ponds from the former iron industry as water features, created his *American* garden. The gardens later came into the ownership of the Loder family where they remained until 2010 when they were sold.

The gardens are famed particularly for Magnolias and Rhododendrons including the *Rhododendron Loderi* named after Sir Edmund Loder. It was Sir Edmund who introduced a variety of animals in 1889 including beavers and mouflons. Of these only the wallabies now remain. The high fence serves equally to keep trespassers out and wallabies confined helping to keep the grassy banks mown. The gardens are no longer open to the public.

> Bear left and after initially following fence line, continue ahead to reach the edge of woodland. Emerge into field and continue ahead to field boundary. Cross second field to meet rough track. Turn left on track and after 100m turn right along field edge.

After 75m turn left and descend on track away from field into woods. Ignore cross tracks, continue descending in woods to where track bears right at a fingerpost. Turn left on path which descends to small footbridge over stream. After crossing bridge reach wide track, bear right. Track bears left and ascends to path junction. Continue ahead on wide track (the right hand track of two ahead), uphill through woods. Path narrows in woods to reach path junction in a clearing. Continue ahead (again the right hand of two paths ahead), to reach stile and lane. Turn left passing *Harvey's Farm* on right. Reach Warninglid Lane, cross and turn right onto verge. After 100m road bears right. Turn left onto enclosed bridlepath which ascends through fields.

Path enters light woodland maintaining same direction, and then follows fields on right to reach house and lane. Continue ahead passing another house on right. Lane descends to reach bridge over the infant River Ouse.

The rust coloured water often seen draining into the stream here is not polluted. The colouring is caused by the iron content of the water.

Continue on lane to reach road. Turn right. Follow road to reach large pond on left (Slaugham Furnace Pond) at crossroads. Turn right and continue on road for about 600m to another bridge over the River Ouse.

The Infant Ouse

On either side of the road at the bridge there are reminders of war: the Second World War. The concrete blocks are anti-tank obstacles. The intention was that tanks would be obstructed or, better still, their vulnerable underbellies exposed to fire if an attempt was made to cross the obstacle. Other reminders of the same war wll be met further down the Ouse.

About 20m beyond bridge turn left over stile through hedge into rough land which can be marshy. Bear half left to reach wooden plank bridge crossing back over river. Two stiles lead into field on right. Continue along left field edge to reach double stile and small wooden footbridge into another field. Cross field diagonally right to reach stile in corner with woodland on right. Follow wood edge to stile and track with water treatment works on right. Immediately beyond entrance to works turn right over stile.

Cross small stream and another stile into field. Continue ahead to reach high wall on right, and stile into road. Cross stile and turn right into **Slaugham** village with church on right.

Slaugham Church

The church is St Mary's. Much of it dates from the 13th century and it is no longer obscured by a public house, the *White Horse*, that stood in front of it between the churchyard and the road until demolished in 1922.

The churchyard holds the tomb of Catherine Matcham, Nelson's younger sister, who lived in the parish with her husband and eleven children. In the church there are also monuments of the Covert family who once lived in nearby Slaugham Place. That great house, now in ruins, lies close to the banks of what is now a slightly larger Ouse and can be reached by a detour through the churchyard. It once housed a great

Unique telephone box in Slaugham Village

household. It was said that the family numbered 70 people but "*family*" in that context meant the whole household, servants and all, not just those related by blood or marriage. One survivor from the ruins is the staircase that is now a bit further down the Ouse Valley in Lewes Town Hall.

Two other things set Slaugham apart: the absence of telephone wires and the white painted telephone box. In the 1930s, Col. Warren, then Lord of the Manor, paid for the wires to be laid underground so that they would not intrude on the village environment. The telephone box was painted white instead of the customary red for the same reason.

The village pump also serves as a reminder that piped water is not a natural occurrence and that the pump was the *chat room* of its day where news and views were exchanged as the buckets were filled.

Misty remains of Slaugham Place

Turn left at road junction and pass *The Chequers* and houses to reach large white gateway. Use side gate to continue in same direction on lane away from village. Remain on lane for about 1,200m passing entrance to *Slaugham Park* on right and metal gates across lane. Reach gate at end of lane and roadway. Cross road and turn left onto footway and reach t-junction and B2110. Turn right and cross road bridge over A23 dual carriageway to village of **Handcross**.

As one ascends the lane towards Handcross, one may, if the day is fair, get a sight over one's right shoulder of the distant Sussex Downs. The authors believe that this is the first sighting of the Downs but, as they had to move that sighting further towards the beginning each time they walked the Way, no prizes are offered for an earlier view.

Turn right at small triangle in road junction and cross road to footpath entrance to *Nymans NT* woodlands through gap in hedge by Handcross village sign.

Nymans is another of the great gardens of Sussex. The estate was bought in 1890 by Ludwig Messel who conceived the garden as a series of *open-air rooms*. With early encouragement from Sir Edmund Loder at Leonardslee, the garden was created, developed and enhanced by three generations of the Messel family even following the gift of the garden to the National Trust in 1953. Further continuity has been given by there being only three head gardeners during the first 100 years. In addition to the gardens at Nymans, open to the public throughout much of the year, there is free public access over the adjoining estate through which the Way passes.

Path descends steeply into woodlands. At cross tracks continue ahead down steps into wood. Track is joined by another from the left and within 20m turn left at a *rustic* fingerpost, (marked *long walk*). With stream on left continue on track and pass through avenue of tall conifers.

Autumn woodland below Nymans

Track bears right and descends to reach lake. Turn right and with lake on left continue ahead. Ignoring first path on left over footbridge reach path junction. Take the left fork retaining sight of lake on left and view of house on hill above lake. Turn left after 35m to cross wooden footbridge over stream, onto duckboards over marshy ground and ascend steps leading to stile into field. Cross field diagonally right to reach a gateway with cattle grid and stile onto concrete lane.

Turn right ascending and then descending to road at **Staplefield Common**, with village green and *Victory Inn* opposite. Cross village green towards cricket pavilion.

Staplefield Common to Lindfield

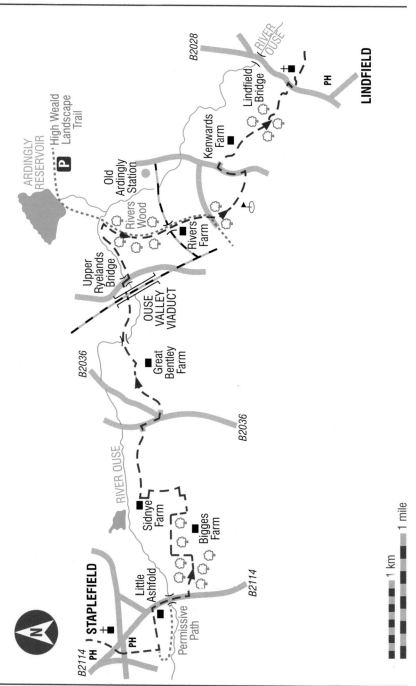

Staplefield Common to Lindfield

Distance – 7½ miles / 12 km

Maps – OS Explorer 134: Crawley & Horsham
OS Explorer 135: Ashdown Forest

"Dear Checker-work of woods, the Sussex Weald!
If a name thrills me yet of things of earth
That name is thine. How often have I fled
To thy deep hedgerows, and embraced each field
Each lag, each pasture – fields which gave me birth
And saw my youth, and which must hold me dead."

Wilfred Scawen Blunt, *from Love Sonnets of Proteus*

The Way continues through the High Weald. It spends more time by the growing river and passes under the Sussex Ouse Valley Viaduct, one of the inspirations of the Way's logo.

To the ancients, water was one of the four elements that together with earth, air and fire, formed the basis of life. This was a view that was not wholly disproved until the eighteenth century and it remains true that water is the major constituent of all living matter, forming from 50 to 90 per cent of living organisms. It is a basic necessity of everyday life without which life cannot exist. Water, and the piping of it into houses, may be taken for granted and expected as some form of right, but that was not always so: the pumps on the greens at Slaugham and Newick serve as reminders of other harder days.

But water provided more. From the earliest of times it provided a means of transport. It is so much easier to make progress even sitting astride a log poling or paddling forward than hacking through the undergrowth. This was applicable to the Weald for, although it was never wholly impassable, there were times when it could only be penetrated on foot with great difficulty and waterborne transport would have presented a much easier option. This was seen on the Sussex Ouse in its most developed form with the navigations that reached from the sea to the site of the Ouse Valley Viaduct and which were originally planned to go higher to Cuckfield.

Water also became the force that drove the mills that lined the banks of the Ouse. Present in Britain since Roman times, water mills, joined by windmills probably after the Crusaders brought the design back from the east, were the stationary engines of their long day driving not just millstones for grinding corn but pumping water from the ground and powering the bellows and hammers for the iron industry. The later steam mills would not have existed without the water and windmills; their wooden machinery was needed in the iron industry to make the metal for the steam engines and the mills that those powered.

The mills that stood on the Ouse give an insight into some of the varied industrial processes that were carried out in the Valley. The Valley contained corn mills and hammer and furnace mills and although most have now gone, names on the map indicate their position and sometimes their varied functions.

As the Way passes south into Lindfield, Fulling Mill Farm lies alongside the river below. Fulling, or felting, was a process in the cloth industry. Newly woven woollen cloth, having first been scoured to remove dirt and grease, was immersed in water and pounded by mechanical means to mat the loose fibres and shrink the cloth to make it weatherproof. Fuller's earth, a source of which was not far across the northern border with Surrey, was used in the scouring. It, and wool, also had their parts to play in that other great Sussex industry – smuggling.

There were a number of paper mills in the valley. These used rags that are still used to make the finest paper although no longer in the Valley. The rags were soaked and pounded to make the pulp from which paper was made. Fine cotton and linen rags were used for white paper for printing and writing. Poorer quality rags were used for the coarse blue or brown papers that were used for packing.

The list of industries in the Valley that used mills goes on. Gunpowder was manufactured; buttons were made; and oil for a variety of uses including lighting and lubrication was obtained from plants such as flax which gave linseed oil.

The biggest local milling enterprise lay at the end of the Way close to the sea from which it received its driving force: Bishopstone Tidemills. Visiting the site with its scattering of low flint walls today it is difficult to envisage that what may have been the largest industrial building in Sussex once stood there.

At one time it housed 16 pairs of millstones and there was a complex of an ancillary windmill, offices, a granary, blacksmith's and carpenter's workshops and a village to house workers and their families who may have numbered as many as 100. When the railway came there was even a station that is now derelict; Bishopstone Station is now a kilometre further on.

The Tidemills were flour mills and were founded in the mid 18th century. In spite of the name the waterwheels were not driven by the tide but by the water flowing back into the sea from mill ponds that had been filled by the incoming tide. The mills were also partly serviced by the sea with barges bringing corn in and taking flour away. Trade declined as competition increased with steam power, more efficient mills and better transport. That decline was aggravated by destructive storms that hit the complex and, finally, the closing in 1884 of the creek on which the mills stood.

The mills never worked after that and were demolished in 1901. The village lived on with a shrinking population. It was joined for a while until the mid 1930s by a racing stable, and the Chailey Heritage Beach Hospital for Crippled Children was also built there. There was also a seaplane base.

The end came with the threat of invasion in the Second World War. The villagers and the children were evacuated and the area cleared to give a field of fire and to remove shelter for invading troops who might succeed in getting ashore.

The mills in the Valley may have had their day but water remains essential. It still has a modern application as a driving force with the need for sustainable sources of power.

To leave **Staplefield Common** village green, cross road by cricket pavillion and enter track.

For many years there was no picture on the sign outside the Victory Inn at Staplefield and the one now there (2012) may seem confusing. A seafaring nation might expect a man of war in full sail with guns ablaze and wonder what the connection might be between Nelson's flagship and an inland rural pub: could it be a celebration of the victory at Trafalgar or from a landlord who had served aboard her, possibly even at the battle?

The name is nothing to do with the sea nor does it commemorate the winners of the clash that took place on the common outside when in 1777 four soldiers unsuccessfully took on a much larger gang of smugglers.

The victory celebrated is a legal one. The Victory was a grocer's shop when a former owner decided to turn part of it into a bar parlour for the sale of alcohol and, after unsuccessful applications to the magistrates for a licence, finally achieved victory and obtained the necessary licence.

Enter field and continue along left hand field edge, gradually descending to kissing gate to enter a small enclosed garden area. Turn left through garden area and pass house, *Little Ashfold* on right onto driveway. Continue to emerge onto B2114 road. Turn right.

Alternative optional route. A Permissive path allows for a short alternative route to reach the B2114 road. Upon reaching garden area cross ahead to another stile into field. Turn right and follow field boundary ignoring stile and small footbridge on right in field corner. Continue around field edge to reach River Ouse on right. Follow the infant river to metal farm gate and wooden plank bridge over river on right in field corner. Turn left away from river along field edge and after 150m turn right through gap into another field. Turn left and follow left hand field edge through two fields, passing pill box, to reach roadway. Turn right.

After about 300m cross River Ouse over road bridge. Cross road and continue with care to brow of hill. Enter footpath on left through metal farm gateway. Follow path with garden on right and descend gradually in woods. Upon reaching another gate enter field and continue ahead along right hand field edge to reach gateway into woods and onto wide, often muddy, track. Exit wood on track to reach farm cottage on right and driveway. Continue ahead on driveway as it ascends towards gateway entrance to *Bigges Farm*. Turn left to gate into field. Turn right and follow right hand field boundary to reach another gate on right and passing *Bigges Farm* house on the right. Pass through gate to reach stile on left into field. Cross stile and follow left hand field boundary. Pass through gateway into another field and continue ahead to gateway and rough track.

Turn left on track which bears right and then left, with large pond on the right. Continue on track towards farm in distance. 100m prior to reaching *Sidnye Farm*, turn left and then right through farmyard to reach house on left. Turn right and pass through other farm buildings, and continue away from farm along farm driveway for about 1km to reach lane. Turn right to B2036 roadway.

Turn left and immediately right into entrance to *Great Bentley Farm*. Continue along farm lane until just before gateway to farm house, turn left through small metal gate.

Descend steps to riverside meadow. Follow path with stream on left. Continue ahead towards a wooden footbridge over River Ouse. Cross bridge and turn half right to cross field towards a large oak tree to reach stile and gateway in corner of field. Cross next field diagonally right ascending to corner and two stiles. Cross into another field and head towards farm buildings. Cross stile by metal farm gate and bear right towards farm cottage. Continue through farmyard with cottage on right. Farm driveway bears left away from cottage. After about 25m turn right over stile in hedge into field. Follow path across field and pass beneath viaduct after crossing two stiles. Head across field to stile and roadway.

The Ouse Valley Viaduct must have been one of the wonders of the Victorian Age. It retains the power to impress today as its 37 arches stride across the valley still supporting the busy schedule of a mainline railway. It is 96 feet high and over a quarter of a mile long: a survivor, it deserves the compliment of imperial measurement rather than the lower numbers of metrication. It also marks the highest point reached by the Upper Ouse Navigation.

Ouse Valley Viaduct

The upper limit of the Navigation was at the wharf opened in 1812 by Upper Ryelands Bridge just short of the Viaduct. Wharf Cottage, built for the wharfinger or manager of the wharf, stands near to the bridge and close to the cottages for the workers building the Viaduct. The 11 million bricks that went into the Viaduct were carried on the Navigation and unloaded at the wharf. These bricks were seeds of the destruction of the waterways. The railways prevailed and inland waterborne traffic went into decline.

River Ouse east of Ouse Valley Viaduct

Turn right on road and cross bridge over River Ouse. Immediately turn left over stile onto path in field beside river. Follow this path and the river passing one wooden footbridge on left to reach second wooden footbridge over river.

For the option to visit Ardingly Reservoir turn left over footbridge and continue over second footbridge before ascending right hand field edge to stile on right. Cross into another field and follow right hand field edge to kissing gate and emerge on high ground above the reservoir. Car park is down slope beneath reservoir dam.

Footbridge near Ardingly

Turn sharp right away from river and footbridge across field towards woods. Enter woods over stile *(High Weald Landscape Trail)* and follow clearly defined path as it ascends through woodland, ignoring several tracks leading off main path. Reach end of wood at wooden farm gate and stile. Cross railway bridge to reach *Rivers Farm*. Pass to left of main farmhouse and cross another stile by gate and follow line of oak trees to reach wooden plank bridge over water course.

The bridge across a railway at Rivers Farm marks the crossing of ways ancient and modern. Centuries before the cutting was excavated for the railway, the Roman London to Brighton road passed diagonally over the ground that once was where the bridge now stands. This was at a point approximately halfway across the bridge. It was not that the Romans discovered the seaside pleasures of Brighton long before the Prince Regent. The road carried iron from local workings but more important was that it was part of a network of roads into London from lands rich in corn further south. The railway below is still in use to transport aggregate. There is another railway reminder 600 metres to the south where the Way meets the road. The embankment that was built for the ill-fated Ouse Valley Railway can be seen on both sides of the road. The proposed route for that railway is later followed for a short distance for it would have lain along what is the drive of Kenwards Farm.

Enter field and continue ahead to reach metal kissing gate and small footbridge over another watercourse. Enter small copse with cottage ahead. Pass to right of cottage and through another metal kissing gate. Follow path through trees with field on right and drive to cottage on left to reach metal kissing gate and emerge onto *Copyhold Lane*. Cross directly to pass through yet another metal kissing gate and enter woodland. Follow clearly defined path as it ascends through wood.

Have some care when suddenly emerging on to the Haywards Heath Golf Course. There is not only the possibility of flying golf balls but also less than happy golfers, concentration disturbed, caught in mid-address of their ball by the unexpected appearance of walkers.

Path emerges from woods onto golf course. Continue ahead on sandy path with tall hedge on right for about 20m. Cross golf fairways to fingerpost in tree line. Bear half left, and follow path through trees, pass through gap in shrubs with house on left, to reach driveway with other houses on left. Continue along driveway *Sandridge Lane* to reach *High Beech Lane*.

Cross road with care and turn left and continue along road for about 300m (care to be taken along this busy road with just a grass verge to walk on). Reach entrance to *Kenwards Farm* on right. Turn into driveway and after about 150m turn right onto a rough track. Track bears left and ascends above *Kenwards Farm* to the left. At track junction bear left, keeping to main track, and descend gradually into woodland. Track narrows to path as it ascends out of woods to reach buildings on right, a gateway and a driveway/path junction. Turn left through gate onto an enclosed footpath to left of bungalow named *Fairlands* and follow, with gardens and houses on right. Path reaches a metal kissing gate and emerges into a gravel courtyard with garages on left. Turn right in courtyard and after 30m turn left to reach High Street at **Lindfield**, opposite the church. Turn right towards village centre. To continue cross road and enter church yard.

The Sussex Ouse Valley Way quickly crosses the upper end of the High Street of Lindfield and passes through the churchyard of the mainly 13th century *All Saints* Church. In the churchyard there is said to be an often quoted epitaph on the headstone of Richard Turner who died in 1768 aged 21 years but who must have been the victim of some earlier catastrophe, or had lingered for a while following surgery:

"Long was my Pain, great was my Grief
Surgeons I'd Many but no relief
I trust through Christ to rise with the just
My Leg and Thigh was buried fust."

According to Ian Nairn and Nikolaus Pevsner in the Sussex volume of *The Buildings of England* (1965) Lindfield High Street, "*is without any doubt the finest village street in East Sussex*" although, due to county boundary changes, it is now in West Sussex. It is certainly well worth a diversion to walk its length. Just down from the church is Church House, formerly the Tiger Inn, parts of which date from the 15th century. Now being in the service of the church, the building has reverted to its former ownership. It was probably the residence for a church dignitary on his visitations to Lindfield. It became an inn after the Reformation in the 16th century. The name, The Tiger, came from a ship owned by the Michelbournes, a family of merchant adventurers. It was in the inn in February 1840 that a meeting of the Proprietors of the Upper Ouse Navigation heard that a "*Rail Way*" was planned in the vicinity. Lindfield was spared the indignity of the "*the tea-kettle with its unmelodious whistle*" that took "*full possession of everything and everybody*" but how many present realised that they were hearing of the beginning of the end of their canal?

Former Tiger Inn, now Church House

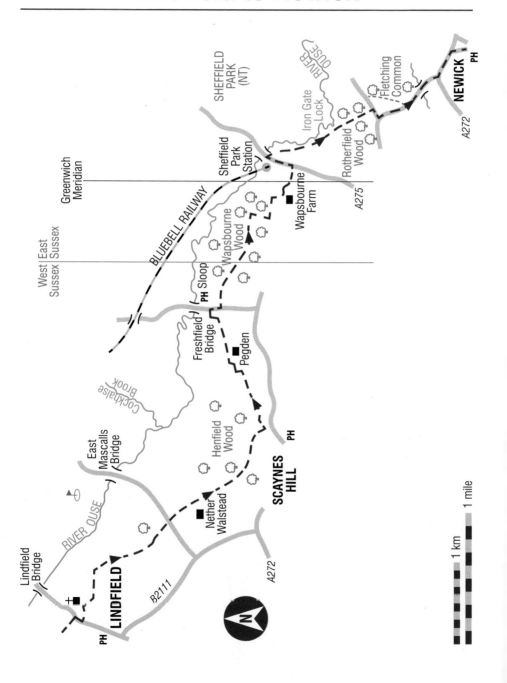

Lindfield to Newick

Lindfield to Newick

Distance – 7 miles / 11 km

Map – OS Explorer 135: Ashdown Forest

And an ingenious Spaniard says, that "rivers and the inhabitants of the watery element were made for wise men to contemplate and fools to pass by without consideration".

Izaak Walton, *The Compleat Angler, first published 1653*

Although never really remote there is a sense of isolation for much of the route as it crosses fields and passes through woodland, travelling over some boundaries on the way. This sense is emphasised by the steam whistles calling from the Bluebell Line but never seeming to intrude.

The difficulties of travelling through Sussex were notorious. The most congested traffic jam on the M25 pales into insignificance against the delays and difficulties that once beset the traveller in Sussex where the mud especially became the stuff of which nightmares are made.

In his book *A Tour through the Whole Island of Great Britain* published between 1724 and 1726, Daniel Defoe wrote… "*on going to church at a country village, not far from Lewis (sic), I saw an ancient lady, and a lady of very good quality, I assure you, drawn to church with six oxen; nor was it done in frolic or humour, but mere necessity, the way being so stiff and deep, that no horses could go on it*".

It may be no more than an early nineteenth century legend that at one time it was necessary to travel from Horsham to London by way of Canterbury, but that may capture a feeling of the frustrations of travel in that area before the improvement of roads by turnpiking.

The situation was no easier for the carriage of animals and goods. Apart from those domestic animals that could provide their own motive power to market and elsewhere by walking there, everything had to be transported in one of three ways: on a man's back; on a pack horse; or drawn by animals either in a wagon or dragged along the ground. That was expensive and only small amounts could be moved and often very slowly. That is unless water power was available: at first along a navigable river and later also along man assisted navigations and man made canals. A navigation is created by making an existing watercourse navigable whereas a canal is a wholly new creation dug from scratch. The men who dug the navigations and the canals were the 'navigators', shortened to 'navvies'.

The golden age of canals can be dated from 1761 when the Duke of Bridgwater opened his canal to carry coal from his collieries to Manchester and covered the years of the Industrial Revolution until overtaken by the railways in the mid-nineteenth century. Coal and raw materials were carried by barge into the mills and manufactured items were carried out the same way from the mills for distribution. The success of canals came from the ease and cheapness for transport in bulk as opposed to the limitations and expense of packhorse or wagon train.

In southern England the manufacturing industries of earlier centuries had passed or were passing into obscurity as the fervour to build canals reached its height. There, apart from some military works, agriculture provided the prime motive to open up the countryside and to carry lime and manure and the latest agricultural methods in to develop poor land and agricultural produce and timber out, although the ubiquitous coal was also a constant cargo.

The canal boom was between 1790 and 1797. The height was in late 1792 and early 1793 not long after the Act of Parliament authorising the Ouse Lower Navigation was passed in 1791. That Navigation was seven miles long from Newhaven to Lewes and partly followed the bends of the river and partly the cuts authorised by the Act.

The Act of Parliament authorising the Upper Navigation was passed a year earlier in 1790 but work took much longer and its working life was considerably shorter than that of the Lower Navigation. The 22 miles with its 19 locks from Lewes to Upper Ryelands Bridge, close by what was to become the Ouse Valley Viaduct, was finally completed in 1812. Stretches had been opened before that date but financial problems as well as the nature of the works contributed to the delay of the whole.

Commercial operations on the Upper Navigation stopped in 1868. By the end of the nineteenth century the locks on the Upper Navigation were in a ruinous state and vegetation was choking the channel.

In contrast, the Lower Navigation continued with regular commercial traffic until 1927 and there was also some commercial use of its lower stretches until the 1950s. It is still in use by pleasure craft today.

In his book *Kent & East Sussex Waterways* first published in 1989, P A L Vine writes of the Upper Navigation, *"The former waterway traverses one of the most beautiful stretches of Sussex countryside and deserves to be restored"*: perhaps this will be so through the efforts of the Sussex Ouse Restoration Trust (SORT).

Upon reaching **Lindfield** High Street turn right and cross road to enter churchyard. Follow path to rear of church and turn right onto rough driveway to Church Close. Follow round to left, passing houses on right and high wall on left. As driveway bears right continue ahead over stile into enclosed footpath. Follow path which remains enclosed but emerges into open land to reach path juction. Turn left and follow to reach farm entrance on left and concrete driveway. Turn right and continue along drive, crossing concrete bridge over stream and passing to side of metal barrier. Before driveway bears right towards farm buildings turn left and enter enclosed path. Path enters wood and crosses footbridge following wire fence on left to another footbridge. Emerge from woods onto tarmac drive with houses on left. Continue ahead towards public road.

About 500 metres after leaving the church at Lindfield, the Way turns right along a concrete driveway and one turns one's back on Hangman's Acre that now lies 100 metres behind. The local gallows was often sited within the jurisdiction of the county sheriff beyond the town boundary and land that was assigned to the executioner either for cultivation or as a place for executions was called *Hangman's Acre*. Status symbols are nothing new. It could also be a matter of prestige. Oliver Rackham points out in his highly recommended *The Illustrated History of the Countryside*, deer parks *"symbolized a higher status than a moat but lower than one's private gallows"*.

Cross road and stile opposite to enter field. Cross left field corner towards stile onto driveway leading to *Nether Walstead*. Cross directly over driveway, over another stile into field and turn half right by large oak tree to cross field towards stile and house. Continue ahead between houses passing to right of wooden garage, towards beech hedge and gap. Cross stile onto rough track and turn left towards fields, passing through gateway. Cross first field to stile in gap. Enter second field and head diagonally left towards woods to reach stile and footbridge into woods. Path bears right, follow through woods to reach fingerpost. Turn left onto path as it ascends through woods to clearing and open scrubland with power lines overhead. Continue ahead and follow wide path along line of power lines through woodland to reach path junction close to the end of the wood. Take left fork through avenue of trees on fence-enclosed path towards house.

Reach driveway and confronted by hedge, turn left and follow drive as it bears right in front of house. Go through kissing gate next to gateway on drive to *Costells* and pass other houses. After about 150m and immediately before reaching road turn sharp left onto driveway leading away from road. On reaching house turn right and cross stile into wide enclosed path to gate into narrower enclosed path. Continue in same direction passing tennis court and house on right, before leaving enclosed path through kissing gate into large field.

Bear half left to cross field to another stile. Enter small copse passing pond on left, to emerge into field. Turn right and follow right hand field edge to pass through gap into another field. Continue in same direction across centre of field on clear path to reach stile. Cross into lane.

Turn left passing *Nash House* on left. Lane bears right and descends towards farm buildings. Turn left before reaching buildings down grass bank onto path through woodland. At stile cross into field. Bear diagonally right to descend field between the centre of two power line posts to reach stile. Cross into woodland and bear left, ignoring the more obvious path off to the right. Follow indistinct path and gully to reach wooden fence and field ahead. Clearer path bears left and follows wooden fencing along left hand field edge to corner of field with house on left. Continue ahead for about 15m to gate. Enter small paddock and turn left. Cross to far right hand corner of narrowing paddock and stile.

Cross onto driveway to *Ham House*, turn right to reach *Freshfield Lane* with *Sloop PH* on left. Turn right along road for 50m, cross and enter drive marked *Bacon Wish* and *Field Cottage* and *West Sussex Border Path*.

If you carry on along the road for about 100 metres instead of turning right into Hammer Wood you reach Freshfield Bridge and the river with the Sloop Inn just before. The Sloop is one of the two inns that lie on the river. Many a pint must have been dispensed to the bargees in the nearly seventy years between the opening of Freshfield Lock in 1799 and its closing in 1868. The lock, of which the chamber is still intact, is upstream from the bridge on the opposite side of the road from the Sloop.

The Sloop

Follow gravel drive passing houses right and left to farm gate into woodland. After about 150m enter light woodland on right and follow ascending path in woodland. Reach stile to emerge into field occasionally used for camping. Cross centre of field towards trees. Turn left remaining in field, passing small pond on right within corner of trees. Continue ahead to cross field to stile and entrance to *Wapsbourne Wood* crossing from West to East Sussex as one passes over the stile.

Although close to the Bluebell Line, Wapsbourne Wood is probably not the scene of the legendary impromptu descents of passengers from the slow moving trains to pick bluebells before straining to get back on board again. But at the right time it can be magical in the radiant blue light of the blooms. And if you get that feeling of being watched, the eyes are probably from one or more of the many Roe deer that usually see you long before you see them. At 24 inches at the shoulder they are not as large as some may think and, if they are not long gone, can easily be missed as they stand stock still amidst the trees.

Wapsbourne Farm – the House

Follow clear path through mainly chestnut woodland, some of which has been recently coppiced, for about 500m to t-junction and track. Turn right onto track and after 40m, turn left onto path which descends gradually in woodland and emerges into field at stile and footbridge. Turn left along left field boundary, cross open field at corner of woodland in same direction to reach stile to right of house. Cross stile into enclosed grass area, turn right to gateway and rough driveway towards Wapsbourne Farm House. Turn left in front of house and continue along driveway leading away from house, crossing bridge over stream and passing more farm buildings on left to reach A275 roadway.

Having already recently passed from West Sussex to East Sussex, the Way now passes from West to East as it crosses the Greenwich Meridian approximately 60 metres short of where the drive of Wapsbourne Farm meets the road.

Cross with care. Turn left along road to reach Sheffield Park Bluebell Line Railway Station on left.

Alternative optional route. A Permissive Path allows for a safer route along road. Turn left before reaching roadway and walk along field edge to a gap in hedgeline on right and steps down to road. Cross with care to grass verge opposite. Turn left to reach Sheffield Park Railway Station on left.

Sheffield Park Station is the southern terminus of the Bluebell Line. The station has been restored in the late 19th/early 20th century style of the London, Brighton & South Coast Railway that originally developed the line that opened in 1882 running between East Grinstead and Lewes and originally known as the Sheffield Park Line: the name *Bluebell Line* came later in the 1950s when a campaign was mounted to save the railway from closure.

If there is a sense of déjà vu when on or about the Bluebell Line, it has appeared in numerous films and television programmes including the second of two versions of E. Nesbit's The Railway Children that both starred Jenny Agutter: as Bobbie Waterbury in the 1970 film version and as Bobbie's mother in the 2001 television version.

The name of the station comes from the nearby great house of Sheffield Park that was the home of the Earls of Sheffield. The house was built in the 18th century for John Baker Holroyd, 1st Earl of Sheffield, by James Wyatt and has gardens that were set out by Capability Brown. The house, a Grade 1 Listed Building, is in private hands.

Bluebell Line

It is now divided into flats one of which was on the market in 2003 for nearly half a million pounds. The National Trust has the gardens which are open to the public.

The title, Earl of Sheffield, has nothing to do with the Sheffield in Yorkshire. There is no anomaly like the Dukes of Norfolk living in Sussex or those of Devonshire in Derbyshire. The Sheffield (sheep land) is from here and the title is purely Sussex.

The first meeting of the Company of Proprietors of the River Ouse Navigation took place under the chairmanship of the first Earl on 17 November 1790 at, appropriately, the Sheffield Arms.

The friendship between Edward Gibbon and the first Earl and Gibbon's burial in Fletching church is more fully mentioned later.

Opposite Station turn right, descend steps to stile into meadow with River Ouse on left. Follow path across field through gates keeping meandering river on left with remains of Iron Gate lock on left. Continue ahead and after crossing small concrete bridge reach stile and wooden gate. Cross small footbridge and turn right after 25m to enter *Rotherfield Wood* on clearly defined path. River bears left and away from route at this point. Track ascends through woods, continue ahead at cross-paths to reach *Mill Lane* through gate.

Turn right to t-junction, turn left and follow road for about 1km, ignoring road on right to reach main A272 road at **Newick**. Turn left to reach village green.

One cannot miss the village pump at Newick. It stands on the village green close by the main road (the A272 that has had an ode written to it) and once will have been one of the focal points of the village dispensing water through the mouth of its head of a handsome lion. There are two signs attached to the pump. One tells us that the pump was, *"Erected by the people of Newick to commemorate the happy completion by Queen Victoria through the grace of God of the 60th year of her good and glorious reign: June 20 1897"*.

The other decrees, *"This pump must not be used for filling steam engines. Any person found damaging this pump will be prosecuted"*.

Steam engines were very thirsty beasts drinking hundreds of gallons of water a day and would have had a disproportionate effect on village resources.

Newick Village Pump

Newick to Barcombe Mills

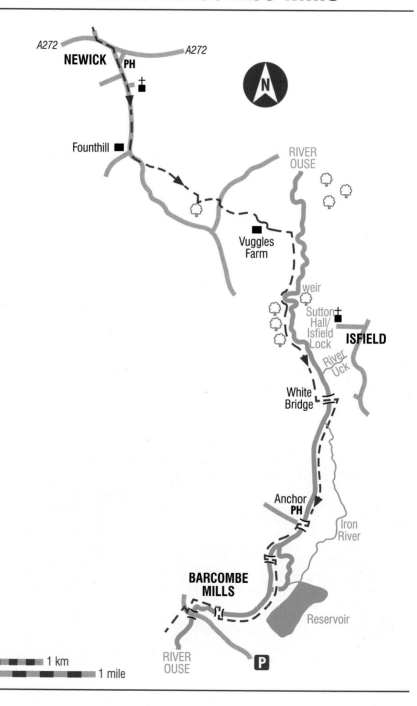

Newick to Barcombe Mills

Distance – 6 miles / 9.5 km

Map – OS Explorer 122: Brighton & Hove

"The prospect is bounded to south-east and east by the vast range of mountains called the Sussex-downs..."

Gilbert White, *The Natural History and Antiquities of Selborne, published 1788*

The countryside becomes more open as the Way advances into the Low Weald. The Way is now more in touch with the river and there is a greater closeness with those who used the river and the navigations and how they were used. But it was the railways that were to prevail.

As schoolboys may know, and those of us who grew up in the last days of almost universal steam railways may remember, the first public steam railway was the Stockton to Darlington. It opened in 1825 and was the harbinger of the onslaught to come.

Investing money in, or sometimes throwing money at, the latest hi-tech revolution, as with the dot.com companies in recent years, is not a modern phenomenon. There had been a canal mania in the late-eighteenth century. This was followed in the nineteenth century by railway mania. There was a rush to invest between the 1830s and 1840s and the railways proliferated. The new era was ushered in amidst a welter of hyperbole from both sides: the romance of horse drawn coaching against the virtues of speed. The enchantment of steam had to wait many years for recognition.

The engineers too were ready and able to go ahead to develop the railways. Civil engineering as a profession had largely been created from the canals with the need to provide accurate and reliable designs, estimates of costs and supervision of works, particularly with the large capital investment that was needed. The development of the design of canals was also in line with the need of the railways. In the main, both preferred a level surface. To achieve that the early canals had followed the contours of the land but to gain a straighter line, cuttings and aqueducts and tunnels were developed to maintain level progress. The skills, in modern jargon, were transferable and they were transferred to the railways.

The railways forged ahead. Canals tried to compete by cutting charges and, in a custom not forgotten, money was spent on dividends not maintenance or capital investment. The railway companies also reduced competition by buying up competing canal companies. And the canals were largely to pass.

The Ouse Valley Viaduct completed in 1841 carried the first steam railway in Sussex but that was and is not the only railway line in or crossing the Sussex Ouse Valley. These include one that never came to life and others that refused to die.

The least sung of the railways in the valley is that which bears or would have borne the name of the valley, the Ouse Valley Railway. But not a rail was laid let alone a train run.

The line that was to run from south of Balcombe to Uckfield and then on to Hailsham was approved in 1864. Work on the track bed was probably started in the following year. Some of the earthworks are still there including an embankment through which the Way passes. The cuttings and embankments are the visible evidence of a political manoeuvre by the London Brighton & South Coast Railway (LBSCR) to combat intrusions into its *territory* by rival railway companies. A truce was, however, agreed between the competing companies in 1866 and work on the line stopped immediately. The LBSCR probably greeted the truce with some relief as that company was having some financial trouble at the time.

The line that linked Lewes to Uckfield, a portion of which is now known as the Lavender Line, was opened on 18th October 1859. Just over a hundred years later it became one of the victims of the Beeching era in the 1960s when the railways were drastically pruned. It finally closed in 1969 after moves apparently to discredit the viability of the line including introducing an unworkable timetable and the substitution of a bus service over part of the line.

Tickets were available from the stations at Barcombe Mills and Isfield. The road at Barcombe Mills was too narrow to be negotiated by a bus, so taxis had to be provided to take passengers to the bus stop further up the line. Travellers could relax in the cushioned comfort of a taxi after their preliminary walk of up to a mile to the station to buy a ticket.

The survival of the Lavender Line is due to the Milham Family that bought Isfield Station in 1983. Track was laid and trains ran again. The line is now operated by a preservation society.

Unlike the Bluebell Line, the Lavender Line is not named after a plant. The truth is, perhaps, more mundane. It takes its name from the coal merchants, A. E. Lavender & Sons who used to operate from the station yard at Isfield.

At **Newick** village green turn right on road and follow south for about 1km, leaving village behind, passing church and *Old Rectory* on left.

The sign outside the Bull Inn at Newick is another where all is not what it seems. Now it shows a fine farm bull but the original bull was a Papal Bull, a formal document issued by the Pope with the heavy leaden Papal seal (the *bulla*) fixed to it. Tradition has it that The Bull, which dates from 1510, was founded for pilgrims travelling between the shrines of St Swithun at Winchester and St Thomas à Becket at Canterbury. It lies almost exactly half way between the two cities. It is not inappropriate that the Way should pass it. The first and most efficacious way to make a pilgrimage was on foot and this is reflected in the Newick Village sign showing a pilgrim's staff clasped in a gloved hand.

On reaching lane on left opposite *Founthill Cottage*, turn left ascending hollow lane until it bears right. Turn left up bank to stile into field. Turn right and pass through gap into second field. Turn left and follow left hand field edge.

Climbing up from the road one reaches the open ridge above Newick. To the north lies the country that has already been crossed and Fletching where the army of Simon de Montfort camped before the Battle of Lewes. Further along the Way there are oast houses to be seen, evidence that hop growing was not confined to Kent but stretched through the Weald into Sussex and beyond into Hampshire where Alton became a home to the brewing industry. To the south, as one passes within a few metres of the short pillar of the Triangulation Point, an essential aid in the accurate plotting of Ordnance Survey maps in the days before satellites, if the day is clear, there is the second sight of the wall of the South Downs stretching from east to west and marking the gateway to the last stages of the journey.

Pass pond on left, continue towards barns to reach farm track. Turn right for about 50m and cross stile on left into field. Follow right hand field edge to reach end of field. Turn right through gate into another field and follow left field edge for 100m to reach post on left. Enter field on left and follow right hand field edge with enclosed wood on right. At end of wood continue across field to metal farm gate into lane.

Turn right on lane for 20m, then turn left up bank to stile into field. Turn left and follow left hand field edge passing wood on left. At the end of wood continue half right across field towards farm buildings. On reaching house on right, pass left, following garden boundary and at end of garden turn right onto grassy track between main farmhouse *Vuggles Farm* on right and old oast house on left. Cross small bridge and watercourse and continue to end of wall and metal farm gate.

River Ouse at Vuggles

Turn left and follow rough track along right hand field edge as it bears right and left. Continue to reach farm gate and stile. Turn right into meadow towards metal farm gate into another meadow passing ox-bow section of the river on left. Cross ditch and turn half right following line of ditch to gap between the river on left and another watercourse on right. Cross middle of next meadow to meet river again after about 250m. Stile on left leads to weir. To continue cross stile ahead on path to pass **Isfield** lock, undergoing restoration, on left.

Until recently Isfield Lock was hidden by foliage. Many a walker on the public footpath that passes close by had no idea that it was there. It is one of those places on the Ouse that now bears scarce trace of the activity that once occurred at what could be described as an "*industrial park*" of its day. There is now no sign of the paper mill or the workers' cottages that once were there.

Weir at Isfield

Remain on path over small footbridge to another stile. Enter open plantation area until path climbs bank to reach stile onto rough track. Turn left and follow for about 300m until gate and stile are reached on left. Cross stile and continue on clear path through several meadows with river on left, to reach stile and *White Bridge* over river. Cross bridge and immediately turn right over stile to continue along east bank of river. Follow river on clear path through meadows. Go through kissing gates immediately before and after walking beneath the old iron railway bridge to continue along river bank to reach kissing gate opposite *The Anchor Inn*.

Perhaps a boat on the river on a warm summer evening dangling a bottle of champagne in the water to cool, but hardly an evocation of the life of a nineteenth century bargee, for the Anchor is another inn opened for the canal trade. It has been said that it has the smallest bar in Sussex which may seem unusual. Built in 1790, the year of the Act of Parliament authorising the Upper Navigation, the *"navigators"* or *"navvies"* with their prodigious thirsts, had yet to pass through. Perhaps it was to discourage their business for the construction gangs were seldom, if ever, welcomed. They often left trails of mayhem, robbery and, sometimes, murder behind them.

Trade declined with the departure in the 1860s of the last barges on the canal and became dependant on local custom. One landlord, seeking to diversify to augment his income, engaged in the once widespread Sussex trade of smuggling for which his licence was confiscated in 1895.

Turn right over concrete bridge and then left away from public house towards automatic water sluices on river. Pass through gate and continue along river bank. After river divides, pass pill box on right before entering enclosed raised path to right of house. Pass through gate and emerge onto tracks with farm buildings and brick bridge on left. Turn right on track to pass barn with corragated roof on left. Almost immediately turn left to pass through *squeeze* stile beside metal farm gate over bridge and cross river again.

The Oil Mills is another place on the Ouse where there is little that shows of all that there once was. The photograph taken in the 1860s shows a substantial mill building three and four storeys high looking solid and permanent: not a trace of that building now remains. What can be traced is the siding that served the mill from the railway that ran close by but which also is no longer there.

The great millstones that lie by the Way are said to have been brought upstream by barge from the Tide Mills. That may be so for John Catt, possibly the son of William Catt, of Tide Mills fame, milled at Barcombe in the 1880s. The linseed oil produced by the mill from grinding flax, also known as linseed, was used as an ingredient of cattle food.

Mill Stones at Oil Mills

Immediately turn right to continue walk along east bank of river. Upon reaching gate, continue ahead on path between two arms of the river. After 50m cross wooden footbridge over river with raised banks of Barcombe Reservoir ahead. Turn right and follow river bank passing the point where the two arms of the river join as one again. Upon reaching reservoir building on left go through gate and continue along river bank in meadow. At another footbridge cross side tributary with pill box on left. Turn right and continue to enter wooded area passing old lock now converted to fish ladders on right and with old *Pikes Bridge* ahead. Cross stile to left of bridge and turn right on to lane to continue.

The letters "NTL" on the Ordnance Survey map show that Barcombe Mills is at normal tidal limit. The river is navigable so far but only for an hour on either

side of high tide; but it is not only boats that come upstream. A clue is in the fish ladders on the stretch of the Navigation that passes under the hump of Pikes Bridge. The answer is given by the notice of the Ouse Valley Angling Preservation Society; daily permits are needed to fish for sea trout between 1st May and 31st October. Each year the sea trout come upstream to fresh water to spawn. There is also a device for counting fish where the old Upper Barcombe Mills lock stood.

To reach large public car park (open summer only) turn left.

Pikes Bridge

Barcombe Mills to Rodmell

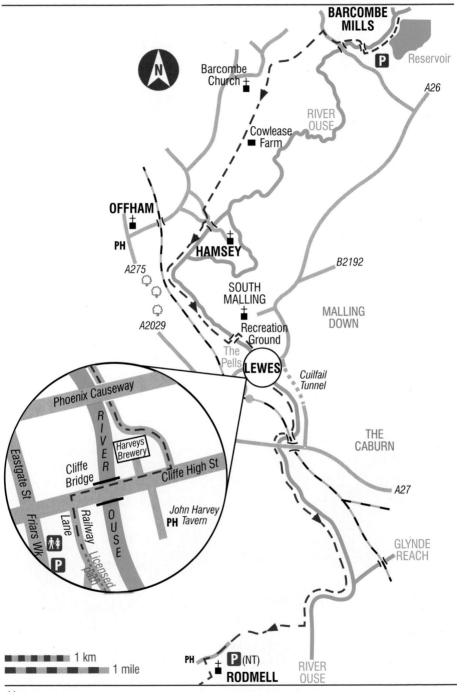

BARCOMBE MILLS

P Reservoir

A26

Barcombe Church †

N

RIVER OUSE

Cowlease ■ Farm

OFFHAM †■

PH

A275

HAMSEY †■

A2029

SOUTH MALLING †■

B2192

MALLING DOWN

Recreation Ground

The Pells

LEWES

Cuilfail Tunnel

THE CABURN

A27

Phoenix Causeway

RIVER OUSE

Harveys Brewery

Eastgate St

Cliffe Bridge

Cliffe High St

Railway Lane

Friars Wlk

John Harvey PH Tavern

P

Licensed path

GLYNDE REACH

1 km

1 mile

PH P (NT)

†

RODMELL

RIVER OUSE

Barcombe Mills to Rodmell

Distance – 8 miles / 13 km

Map – OS Explorer 122: Brighton & Hove

"Then times be rude and weather be rough,
And ways be foul and fortune tough,
We are of stout South Country stuff,
That never can have good ale enough...."

Hilaire Belloc, *from The Four Men*

A section of contrasts: the Way shadows the now navigable river as it flows out of the Low Weald and through the South Downs taking in the historic town of Lewes, the only inland town en route.

There are signs of conflict and scenes of battle for once you have got there, supplanting earlier inhabitants, and settled it to your liking, there is usually somebody who wants to take it away from you. There are many signs of successive waves of invasion through the valley of the Sussex Ouse. Within little more than the last two thousand years there have been the Celts, the Romans, the Saxons and, in the last successful invasion of England, the Normans. There are also signs of a couple that did not make it.

Each has left their mark on the landscape in one way or another, some fainter than others. In the valley little visible remains of the Romans and Saxons, each overcome by succeeding invasions, but on the Way, what were once the site of Roman roads are crossed and re-crossed and the names that the Saxons left spread across the map. Amongst the most obvious signs of the Celts are iron age hillforts dominating heights of the South Downs but, as some would have us believe, the history of civilised England did not begin until the invasion in 1066 by the Normans who built the looming presence of Lewes Castle, the strategic position of which can be appreciated by standing on Southease Bridge and looking northwards.

There was actually civilisation in England before that date but to the victor lies the spoils of propaganda.

When they came, the Normans divided Sussex, the kingdom of the South Saxons, and the county where the Normans first landed, into six territorial divisions called Rapes: the Rapes of Hastings, Pevensey, Lewes, Bramber, Arundel, and Chichester. No other county was divided in the same way. Each Rape had a port and strong castles to control the way northward and to defend the ports to secure communications with and supplies from Normandy and, possibly, to provide escape routes back to Normandy if need arose. These Rapes were entrusted by William to his most trusted barons. Rape most probably comes from an old Norse word for rope and the Normans were descended from the Vikings. It is used in that sense in Bosham, a Sussex haven for yachtsmen, where the Raptackle, an ancient wooden building, is still used for storing ropes and tackle.

And ropes were used for measuring. In Britain a 'cable' was one tenth of a nautical mile. The story also goes that Richard Fitzgilbert, one of the leading followers of William the Conquerer in 1066, measured the boundaries of his castle at Brione with a rope so that he could check to see that he was getting as much as he was giving up. He could not have been dissatisfied for his reward was nearly 200 English manors spread across 8 counties.

Home grown conflicts also echoed through the Valley. The most important of these was the Battle of Lewes that took place on 14 May 1264 when baronial forces under Simon de Montfort defeated the royalist forces of King Henry III and the King's son Prince Edward, later Edward I, the Hammer of the Scots. This lead to a form of government by council but that and De Montfort's triumph of defeating the superior royalist forces was short lived. He was killed in the following year. He would probably have been surprised that the Victorians credited him as the founder of democratic parliamentary government. His intent was to curb royal power to gain control for himself, not for the people.

But raiders still came ashore; usually the French who raided along the Sussex coast for centuries, burning and looting. In 1377 they marched on Lewes, capturing the prior of Lewes Priory who had been leading the resistance to them. But the raiding was not entirely one sided nor always successful. The compliment was often returned, sometimes on a much larger scale. One such English raid culminated in the Battle of Agincourt in 1415 and a plaque close to the end of the Way tells how in 1545 Sir Nicholas Pelham organised resistance to and routed the French forces that two days earlier had taken part in the engagement during which the great warship and pride of the English fleet, Mary Rose, sank; the Mary Rose that was raised from the seabed in 1982 and whose timbers are now preserved at Portsmouth.

Napoleon was one who did not make it. In the end he did not set sail but preparations were made to receive him if he had. The cookhouse from Horsham Barracks now stands at the main entrance to Leonardslee and, a little further on from the end of the Way, there is the Martello Tower at Seaford, one of a string of small forts that was built along the south and south-eastern coasts to greet his forces should they come. Each was capped by a gun platform with usually only one single heavy cannon but that was able to swivel in a 360° degree arc. Some saw later service as stations of the Coast Blockade that was formed in 1817 to combat smuggling, but without the cannon.

Newhaven played a vital role in both World Wars. Between 1914 and 1918 it was the principal supply port for the Western Front in France with an average of a supply train arriving every 30 minutes both day and night throughout the four years of war. In World War II it was the principal base for the ill fated raid on Dieppe in 1942 and was a major port used in the D Day invasion of 1944. Newhaven Fort, set into the chalk of the headland above the harbour, saw service in both wars but was originally built in the 1860s to defend against invasion, the perceived enemy then being the French.

Throughout the Valley there are further reminders of World War II and another would-be invader who did not make it. These include the anti-tank blocks close to Slaugham and the increasing number of pill boxes that are encountered as one travels southwards, so much so that Barcombe Mills was christened *Pill Box Alley*.

Pill boxes are sometimes more officially known as defence posts, blockhouses or police posts. Most of those in England date from 1941, when over 18,000 were built. The pill boxes in south east England formed part of the anti-invasion defences when it was believed that enemy advances would be by tanks supported by infantry. The boxes were intended to disrupt and delay any advances that might have broken through the coastal defences before those advances hit the inner defences further north towards London. The boxes are of an extremely strong construction and many remain in the countryside due to the difficulty of demolishing them.

Each generation hopes that war and invasion will never come again and, in Sussex, that '*Silly Sussex*' will remain at peace. But those who live in Sussex know that they are not intellectually challenged. '*Silly*' is a corruption of a

Saxon word *Sælig*, meaning happy or blessed. The Saxons when they came, thought that the local inhabitants were of such a happy spirit.

Crossing Pikes Bridge follow lane as it bears left and right over other bridges passing several water courses and ponds. When lane reaches houses and entrance to *Barcombe House* on right, turn left to reach public road. Turn right and pass old **Barcombe Mills** railway station on left.

Barcombe Gin

As the name suggests Barcombe Mills is another of those industrial complexes of which little trace now remains. The mill was directly served by water, rail and road transport and after a mixed history as a corn mill and, for a while, to make buttons from imported nuts, burnt down in 1939. In the Second World War the road alignment was altered and a new bridge constructed over the river that bypassed the ancient toll bridge the tariff for which is still displayed by the Way.

As road bears right and ascends turn left over stile into field next to pill box. Follow left field edge to stile into second field. Continue ahead following left field edge to third stile. Cross and follow path to another stile and footbridge into orchard, to reach footbridge over ditch. After 30m cross line of old railway and reach another stile into a large field. Cross centre of field to fingerpost to left of tree line and another large field. Bear half right and cross field towards house. Pass through gate into fenced paddock. Cross to fingerpost and turn left into enclosed footpath which emerges firstly onto drive to house named *Wychwood*, then onto lane.

Cross lane into large field and follow right field edge with trees on right. Continue ahead with views of Barcombe Church on right.

Alternative optional route. To visit church turn right at lane and bear left to reach another lane and church entrance on left. On leaving church turn right through gate into field and cross diagonally right to stile and plank bridge over ditch rejoining the route.

Continue ahead on right field boundary to reach concrete bridge over watercourse into another field with farm buildings ahead. Pass through farmyard. When farm driveway bears right, away from farm, continue ahead on grass to right of houses and hedge to emerge into large field. Cross centre of field maintaining same direction. Pass over ditch into yet another large field and continue across centre of field to reach line of trees on right field edge. Continue ahead on enclosed and initially sunken path within trees to reach lane. Turn left and follow lane through village of **Hamsey** to reach *Hamsey Place Farm* entrance on left over bridge which crosses River Ouse *Hamsey Cut*. Leave road and continue ahead on rough grass track.

Hamsey Church

Once the village of Hamsey clustered round the church on its narrow hill. It was no doubt there that the Saxon King Athelstan held the Gemote, a meeting of his counsellors, in 925 AD and where, in the early 14th century, a great hall was built for the de Says whose family name contributed the SEY to Hamsey. But the village slipped away. There are several reasons why villages edged sideways or disappeared altogether. Plague is the one that seems first to spring to mind, sometimes with stories of self sacrifice as stricken villagers withdraw from the surrounding world to avoid spreading the disease. There was also famine. Some were moved to improve the view of the landowner. The reason, as here, could be more prosaic. The village could not expand on the narrow hilltop and the valley floor below was liable to flooding. The valley slopes were used instead.

Offham Hill lies to the west above the Way. On 14 May 1264 the army of the rebel barons under the command of Simon de Montfort appeared on top of Offham Hill. It was about 5000 strong with 600 cavalry and was outnumbered 2 to 1 by the Royalist forces below in Lewes. The King must have known that the rebels were nearby but he was denied news of their arrival as the only Royalist look-out posted on the hill was captured asleep.

Memorial to the Battle of Lewes in grounds of Lewes Priory

Battle was joined: Prince Edward based on the castle in command of the Royalist right charged the rebel left wing in advance of the other Royalist forces. The left wing consisting of scarcely trained and badly armed Londoners was routed and put to flight down into the Ouse Valley where the Way runs.

Hundreds died as Edward and his soldiers engaged in an unruly pursuit. Behind him the remainder of the two armies clashed. By the time Edward returned Simon de Montfort and the rebels had prevailed. The Royalist forces had been defeated. Edward's absence had been decisive in the defeat of his own side. It was not a mistake that he was to repeat in the future.

Follow line of Hamsey Cut on rough track and embankment, passing through gate and passing the remains of *Hamsey Lock* on left to where Hamsey Cut rejoins the river. Continue ahead following river to reach railway bridge and a double squeeze stile on left. Pass through, and continue to follow river towards **Lewes** town with railway on right. After about 800m houses and church of South Malling can be seen on opposite side of river. Upon reaching metal footbridge, Willeys Bridge, on left and path junction, cross river by bridge and turn right to continue to follow river in parkland. *Tesco* store is passed on left. Continue on path by river to *Harvey's Brewery*.

While much of the industry has gone from the river, Harveys is now in its third century and seventh generation in Lewes as an independent family brewer having survived flood, fire, pestilence and take over bids.

Harveys Brewery, Lewes

Having brewed in Lewes for some years, Harveys came to the banks of the Ouse when John Harvey (1784-1862) bought the Bridge Wharf site where the brewery still stands in the late 1830s. The river served the brewery with deliveries in and out. The present Victorian listed building was started in 1881 although the equipment that it now houses is modern.

Pestilence struck in 1875. The contaminated municipal water supply caused a typhoid epidemic in which 30 people died. A bore hole sunk on site revealed an alternative source of clean, fresh water 60 feet below that still supplies the brewery.

Serious flooding has disrupted the brewery on occasion. The last was in October 2000 when the brewery was overwhelmed by up to eight feet of water but by a supreme effort brewing was resumed in nine days to the relief of many a customer. Harveys has a warm spot in the heart of any Sussex beer drinker and its renown spreads beyond the county boundaries having won an international reputation and many an award for the quality of its beers.

Path bears left and then right to emerge onto Cliffe High Street in Lewes.

Following his success in invading England in 1066 William the Conqueror entrusted the Rape of Lewes to William de Warenne. In 1077 de Warenne and his wife, Gundrada, sometimes reputed to be the Conqueror's daughter, founded the Priory of St Pancras at Lewes. The Priory grew over the following centuries with a church nearly 450 feet long and, it is said, 100 monks at the height of its success. The end came in 1537 with the dissolution of the monasteries by Thomas Cromwell under Henry VIII when the remaining 23 monks and their 80 servants departed. The Priory and all its lands were granted to Thomas Cromwell. In the following year, on the orders of Cromwell, an Italian named Portinari, with the assistance of gunpowder, made a sweeping destruction to the intent that all should be levelled. Local legend has it that the Sussex marble altar stone from the Priory church was cast into the Ouse somewhere between Cliffe Bridge and where the railway now crosses the Ouse but it has never been found. Could it be that it was saved by those who kept to the old faith and secreted elsewhere? The large memorial brass to Thomas Nelond, the 26th prior, that presumably also had been in the Priory church, is now in the church at Cowfold in West Sussex.

Looking south from Cliffe Bridge, Lewes

…and the same view in 1898

Turn right and cross Cliffe Bridge and river again. After 20m turn left into Railway Lane passing car park and toilets on right. When road bears right continue ahead on side road towards old railway crossing gates. Upon reaching the gates bear left onto riverside path through scrubland. Follow this licensed path along river bank with water meadows on right passing through several squeeze stiles for about 1km until the path meets the railway bridge over the river.

Just south of where Railway Lane passes into the Railway-land Nature Reserve, the Winterbourne flows into the Ouse: or does at a certain times of the year for winter bourne is descriptive. The stream flows mainly in the winter. The *bourne* comes from the Old English. It means stream and, probably more specifically, a stream with clear water in chalk country or with a gravel bed. There is also the word *bourn* which in Southern England, particularly in chalk country, means a stream that, like the Winterbourne, flows intermittently but the derivation is later. The Winterbourne is both *bourne* and *bourn*.

The large fish sometimes seen congregating at the mouth of the Winterbourne are mullet not sea trout on their way upstream.

The Snowdrop Inn lies on the other side of the river beneath the white chalk face that is beginning to disappear beneath a cover of greenery. The snowdrop is not of the botanical kind. It may seem incongruous but Britain's greatest snow avalanche disaster happened here in Sussex in the south east of England.

Snow had fallen heavily in the Christmas week of 1837. Gales had caused drifting. This formed, according to one newspaper report, a *"continuous ridge of snow from 10-15 feet in thickness along the brow"* of the height above where the Snowdrop Inn stands, *"where tons and tons seemed to hang in a delicately turned wreath as lightsome as a feather but which, in fact, bowed down by its own weight, threatened destruction to everything beneath"*: a cornice. A preliminary fall gave warning of what was to come but it seems largely to have been ignored. The inevitable happened. Six people were rescued but eight, ranging in age from 15 to 82, perished when the Poor House below was engulfed.

Mount Caburn dominating the skyline east of the river

Pass through kissing gate and continue on river bank under bridge. Path briefly bears right away from river before returning to the river bank to pass beneath road bridge.

Continue along riverside raised bank for about 2.5km. Cross two stiles next to Rodmell Pumping Station and continue for another 200m to reach another stile and fingerpost. Do not cross stile but turn right down embankment onto rough track. Follow track through farm gates to reach road and the houses of **Rodmell** village. Pass National Trust car park on left, continue along street to reach path to school and Rodmell church on left immediately after passing *Monks House*.

Rodmell to Seaford Bay

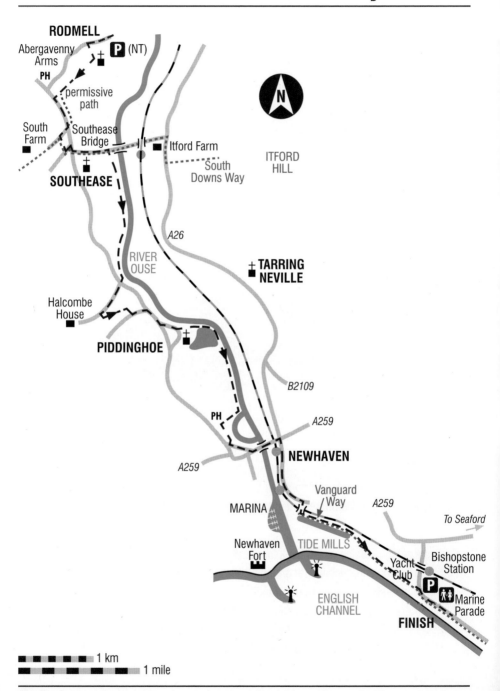

RODMELL

Abergavenny Arms

PH

permissive path

P (NT)

South Farm

Southease Bridge

Itford Farm

SOUTHEASE

South Downs Way

ITFORD HILL

N

A26

RIVER OUSE

TARRING NEVILLE

Halcombe House

PIDDINGHOE

B2109

PH

A259

A259

NEWHAVEN

Vanguard / Way

A259

To Seaford

MARINA

Newhaven Fort

TIDE MILLS

Yacht Club

Bishopstone Station

P

Marine Parade

ENGLISH CHANNEL

FINISH

1 km

1 mile

Rodmell to Seaford Bay

Distance – 6½ miles / 10.5km

Map – OS Explorer 122: Brighton & Hove

*"… where windy Piddinghoe's
Beguilded dolphin veers
And red beside wide-bankéd Ouse
Lie down our Sussex steers"*

Rudyard Kipling, *Sussex, 1902*

The river reaches the sea at Newhaven, the port that was new in the 15th century when a cut was made for the river to take a shorter route to the sea. The Way then continues for another two kilometres following the old course of the river and on to meet the sea at Seaford Bay.

Although memories of conflict have not been left behind, the valley of the Sussex Ouse is peaceful and remains an attraction to those who use words rather than force.

The concept of comprehensive universal education is relatively modern. It was, perhaps, received with general enthusiasm and observance in rural areas somewhat later than elsewhere. Money could not be earned at school. Even pence brought in by the young could make a significant difference to a borderline standard of living. Lack of facilities, however, did not denote a lack of desire for education nor was it impossible to overcome. One who did was John Dudeney.

Born in 1782 in Rottingdean, his formal education was limited to a few weeks at a dame school from which he was removed by his parents lest the close proximity of a stretch of water should be the end of him instead of the school providing a foundation for life. His parents having some literacy were able to teach him the basics of reading, writing and arithmetic.

Starting work looking after sheep at the age of eight and later becoming a shepherd at Kingston near Lewes, he was nevertheless driven by a thirst for learning. Much of his small income was spent on books that he kept in a hole covered with a stone that he had dug on Newmarket Hill that he called his *"understone library"*. He must have been one whose glass is half full for, on finding that he had by mistake spent some of his hard earned money on an apparently useless book in French, he turned that to advantage by buying a Grammar and a French-English Dictionary and taught himself that language. High on the Downs in the company of his sheep, he also taught himself Hebrew so that he could read the bible, *"that most interesting of all books"*, in the original and mastered algebra, geometry and astronomy. He built his own telescope too.

He left the sheep to work for a publisher in Lewes, later becoming a respected schoolmaster who started his own school and took a leading part in the foundation of the Lewes Mechanics Institute.

Some years earlier, Lewes had been the home of Thomas Paine (1737-1809) for six years from 1768 where, somewhat surprisingly for a developing radical, he served the government as an exciseman, although dissent was no stranger to Lewes. Monks from Lewes had negotiated with the Crown on behalf of Simon de Montfort following his defeat of the Royalist forces at the Battle of Lewes leading to a treaty that may have laid the foundations for parliamentary government; 17 Protestants had been burnt at the stake in the Market Square during the reign of Mary I, *"Bloody Mary"*; the town had supported Parliament during the English Civil War; and the nonconformist past of Lewes is still commemorated today on Bonfire Night, 5th November, with the cries of, *"No Popery"*.

Service in Washington's continental army on the American side during the American Revolution, the publication of the seminal *Rights of Man*, indictment for treason and being a member of the French National Assembly during the French Revolution, all lay in the future. In Lewes Paine developed and matured and honed his talents partly at the debates of the Headstrong Club that met in that wood panelled room still there on the first floor of the White Hart opposite the Law Courts in the High Street.

He did not endear himself to the Board of Excise when in 1773, at the invitation of his fellow officers, he was the author of a memorial to parliament seeking improvement in pay and time spent away from his post promoting the memorial cost him the post. He was discharged by the Board of Excise for, *"having quitted his Business, without obtaining the Board's leave for so doing"*. His property had to be sold by auction to pay the debts that he had accumulated.

In 1774 he sailed for the American Colonies following that earlier emigrant, John Harvard, who had married at South Malling close to Lewes in 1636 and who, in his will, left the sum of £779 and 300 books to the new college at Cambridge, Massachusetts later to be named after him.

Another facet of the eighteenth century, away from the turmoil of revolution, reflects the elegance and studied reason of that age as shown by that monumental work, both history and literature and surely a necessity for desert islands, *The Decline and Fall of the Roman Empire* by Edward Gibbon (1737-1794) that was published in 6 volumes over a period of 12 years between 1776 and 1788.

Due to financial circumstances Gibbon spent the later part of his life in Lausanne but on hearing of the death of Lady Sheffield, the wife of his friend John Baker Holroyd, the first Earl of Sheffield, he returned to England and spent the summer of 1793 at Sheffield Park. From there he went to London, fell ill and, after two operations, died in January 1794. The Earl had Gibbon's body interred in the Earl's family mausoleum in Fletching Parish church just outside Sheffield Park.

When John Dudeney was tending his sheep James Hurdis was Rector at the inland village of Bishopstone. He had been born there in 1763. He was educated at Chichester and Oxford and, after a period as curate at Burwash, returned to Bishopstone as Rector in 1791 until his early death in 1801 at the age of 38. In 1793 he was elected professor of poetry at Oxford. He was a friend of the poet William Cowper, best known for *The Diverting History of John Gilpin*, and a poet in his own right. Amongst his works is *The Favourite Village* that, in the words of Peter Brandon "... *combines his love of his native place of Bishopstone ... with a celebration of God's divine creation of the Ouse Valley*".

Charles Dickens was a visitor to Lindfield. He stayed at a house called *Foyles* in the High Street and helped his friends, the Smiths, to build *The Chalet*.

A somewhat less happy stay was spent by Tennyson a little further north in the Ouse Valley at Warninglid near Slaugham to which he came as a newly married man in about 1850. According to one less than wholly reliable source he was last seen in Warninglid pushing his wife in a bath chair along the rough road to Cuckfield. But undoubtedly there were problems. Part of the bedroom wall was blown down in a storm letting in the wind and rain.

They learnt that part of the house had been a Roman Catholic Chapel: that a baby was buried somewhere in the house: that the *Cuckfield Gang*, notorious murderers and thieves, had lived in the lodge. No postman called and no carrier passed within hailing distance. The nearest doctor and butcher were 7 miles away in Horsham.

Tennyson did return to Sussex but not to the Ouse Valley. From 1869 until his death in 1892 he lived at *Aldworth* a house that he had built for him on Black Down, the highest point in Sussex, away from the prying eyes that had bedevilled his life on the Isle of Wight; the cult of celebrity is nothing new.

In more recent years, the Bloomsbury Group, made their mark, sometimes literally, in and about the Ouse Valley. The Group's name came from the salon hosted by the sisters, Virginia and Vanessa Stephen at their Bloomsbury flat that was frequented by artists, writers and philosophers. In 1912, Virginia married Leonard Woolf and they moved into the Ouse Valley by taking a lease on *Asham House* on the lower slopes of Itford Hill looking across the valley. In 1919, their landlord needed the house for his farm bailiff and the Woolfs moved to Rodmell on the other side of the Ouse where they bought *Monks House* at auction for £700.

Monks House

Poppies above the Ouse Valley

Both houses were a centre for the Bloomsbury Group. Leading figures of the age came to stay including T S Eliot, Maynard Keynes, the economist, Lytton Strachey, E M Forster, Stephen Spender, Vita Sackville-West and many others. Virginia Woolf's fame and success as a novelist increased during her time at *Monks House* where some of her best known works were written including *Mrs Dalloway* and *To the Lighthouse*.

Virginia Woolf is regarded as one of the leading and most innovative novelists of the twentieth century but she suffered from recurrent bouts of depression and mental illness. It was during the course of one of those that she made her way down to the bank of the river. Leaving her stick she entered the water, a large stone in her pocket. Her body was found three weeks later.

Asham House is no longer there but *Monks House* now belongs to the National Trust and is open at certain times of the year.

Although painted after Virginia Woolf's death, the paintings on the walls of Berwick Church by her sister Vanessa Bell, Quentin Bell and Duncan Grant are a vivid reminder of the onetime presence of the Bloomsbury Group in the Ouse Valley.

Although sadly the Ouse Valley was to be the scene of the ending of Virginia Woolf's life in 1941, Monks House was a home for her and her husband, Leonard Woolf, who stayed on until his death in 1969, providing a retreat from London as Sussex has done, and still does, for many.

There is a strong walking connection through Virginia Woolf. Her father was Sir Leslie Stephen (1832-1904): scholar, critic, publisher and mountaineer. In 1897 when his more active mountain days were done, he founded one of the earliest walking groups, *The Sunday Tramps*, the membership of which was strictly controlled by him and consisted mainly of distinguished intellectuals. Every other Sunday, for about eight months of the year, they covered between 14 to 20 miles across country in the countryside around London from one railway station to another. Their favoured territories were the Chilterns and the North Downs. They were not averse to trespass when needed and the formula, delivered in chorus, when challenged was *"We hereby give you notice that we do not, nor doth any of us, claim any right of way or other easement into or over these lands, and we tender you this shilling by way of amends."* It is said sometimes to have worked but neither practice is now recommended.

Walking west through **Rodmell** village pass *Monks House NT*, and turn left from street towards school and church. Enter churchyard through lychgate and continue ahead following wall on right to corner and steps over wall. Continue ahead and follow path along rear of house and converted barn to track leading to road.

Alternative optional route. To continue through Rodmell remain on road after passing Monks House. On reaching main road and The Abergavenny turn left for about 150m to rejoin route.

The Way joins the South Downs Way and follows it for a little over a kilometre past Southease Church as far as Southease Bridge. The South Downs Way is a National Trail and as such is marked with the acorn symbol. Originally opened in 1972 it now stretches some 100 miles (161km), depending on your source, from Eastbourne in East Sussex to Winchester in Hampshire. It was also the first long distance bridleway to be opened in Britain and as such caters for a wide range of users. It mainly follows the escarpment of the Downs and if the day is fair can give sweeping and spectacular views over the Weald to the north, the sea to the south and the Isle of Wight.

The blacksmith's forge stands opposite the Abergavenny Arms. When the McCarthys were researching the second volume of their book Sussex River that was published in 1977 they met the blacksmith, Frank Dean. In 1956 he had succeeded his father who had taken the forge over in 1910. Frank Dean was still working at the forge in 2004. Sadly he died in July of that year aged 87 after having put in a full day's work but he is succeeded at the forge by his son and grandson.

Turn left along road for about 250m, cross road and enter track to *South Farm*. As track bears right turn left onto path *South Downs Way*. After passing through gateway reach fingerpost, turn left ascending to top of field and gate to road. Turn left, cross main road again, turn right and then left into road to **Southease**.

Alternative recommended route. Immediately before reaching main road turn left on enclosed permissive path following right field boundary and line of road. Path bears left to reach gate. Pass through gate turn right to reach road at Southease. Turn left.

The church of St Peter at Southease is one of the three in Sussex with a round tower. They are all in the Ouse Valley. Of the other two, one is in Lewes and the third a little further downstream at Piddinghoe. There are several theories why the towers should be round but in the days when the towers were built local materials were generally used as transport difficulties made the import of better building stone prohibitive for more than the most prestigious of buildings: castle or cathedral but not a humble local church. Here the local building material was flint.

Southease Church

In his book *The South Downs*, Peter Brandon suggested that this is the reason for the round towers. Flint is not found in large pieces and so it is difficult to build square shapes without additional support at the corners.

Descend through Southease on lane passing church and small green on right towards river and Southease Bridge. Do not cross river, turn right through gate onto riverside path.

Southease Bridge

The grade II listed bridge that crosses the Ouse at Southease was originally built in 1791. It was rebuilt in the 1880s and restored in 2010 at a cost of £1.7m. It was built as a swing bridge to let river traffic pass through but had not operated as such for many years. Although the turntable was replaced in 2010 the opening mechanism was not and there are no plans to do so. In the end age defeats many a former swinger.

Follow path on raised bank for about 1.5km when the path converges with roadway. Cross stile into road and cross with caution to enter driveway through large entrance gateway which immediately passes to the left of a converted barn. Continue on track for about 600m and turn left off track at fingerpost and ascend grass bank to gateway. Follow path as it bears left along hillside and then follows low wall to gateway. Through gate turn left onto metalled lane. Descend on lane to reach roadway.

The round tower of the church at Piddinghoe supports a gilded weather vane surmounted by a sea trout rather than the dolphin of Kipling's verse.

There is another verse about Piddinghoe:

> *"Englishmen fight, Frenchmen too:*
> *We don't, we live at Piddenhoo."*

This may show a very human wish to keep one's head down and get on with life untroubled by the outside world particularly if one was in the middle of warring parties and, war or not, if one of one's major occupations was smuggling.

Piddinghoe Church

It may also have been through this isolation that a number of stories circulated about the village and who is to say that the village did not discourage those stories to preserve that isolation. It was said that those at Piddinghoe engaged in some peculiar occupations. They hung their fields out to dry. They fished for the moon and dug for moonshine. They shod magpies.

The fields were hung out to dry as one of Piddinghoe's industries was making whitening by grinding chalk in water and then spreading it on sloping shelves to dry. Fishing for the moon or digging for moonshine was dragging a pond for or digging up concealed smuggled goods. Shoeing magpies may have been shoeing black and white oxen that were used for ploughing. Those would not have been the *Sussex steers* also mentioned by Kipling. Sussex cattle are a rich red colour.

Until 1912 a normal occupation that was carried on at Piddinghoe was brick making. A restored kiln can be seen in the village. Many bricks from Piddinghoe were shipped upstream to become part of the Ouse Valley Viaduct that would carry the railway that helped the decline of the canal trade.

Turn right and after 50m cross and turn left on side road into **Piddinghoe** village. Upon reaching millennium memorial and with church ahead, turn left onto riverside path. Follow riverside path for about 1.5km towards Newhaven docks and boatyard.

Newhaven is a working port. It makes no pretence to be otherwise. It also has a distinct advantage over many other ports. With the sea to the south it is otherwise surrounded by high white cliffs, the rolling green topped, round headed Sussex Downs (but Kipling put it much better) and the Ouse Valley stretches into the green fields and woods of the Weald that many consider to be the quintessence of England.

Writing in 1904, E V Lucas, the doyen of Sussex travel writers, was not kind to Newhaven but one who was glad to see Newhaven was Louis-Philippe, King of the French. He had been ousted from power in one of the popular revolutions that swept across Europe in 1848. He landed at Newhaven to be welcomed by William Catt of the Tide Mills who had advised him in France. The Way passes close to the Bridge Hotel where Louis-Philippe and his Queen registered under the names of Mr and Mrs Smith, pseudonyms that in later years might have given rise to misunderstandings.

As you cross the bridge over the Ouse, look to the south towards the ferry terminal and the sea for our favourite cormorant posing. Is it purely a coincidence that the wreckers from Seaford who lured ships to their doom were nicknamed 'Cormorants' or 'Shags' which are a smaller Cormorant-like bird.

Path bears right away from river alongside boatyard. Keeping right of wire fence descend off bank to path towards playing fields on right with water ditch between. On reaching first road, turn left passing flats then rear of houses on right. At the gate entrance to the Lewes District Council yard turn right into narrow enclosed footpath which bears left and passes between yard and rear of houses to emerge onto footway and main road.

Estuary at Newhaven

Turn left on footway, passing subway on right, to reach to roadside pavement. Continue ahead ignoring road bridge on left to *Denton Island* to reach main road bridge over river. Cross road by pedestrian lights and turn left onto bridge crossing river. Descend on sliproad pavement from main road. Cross road leading to ferries to level-crossing.

Cross railway line and turn right into Railway Road. Continue along road, which becomes Beach Road, for about 750m, passing **Newhaven** Harbour Station on right. As road bears left turn off right onto footpath beside wire fence, marked *Sussex Ouse Valley Way* and *Vanguard Way*. Cross footbridge over railway and remain on path towards **Seaford** passing Mill Creek on right, with railway on left. Pass through remains of the Tide Mills.

Tide Mills

There is now almost no sign, apart from a deserted railway station, of the community that once lived and worked at the Tide Mills. The village of Bishopstone is still there less than a mile inland to the north east. It stands about its church dating from Saxon times with the sundial on its tower created by or dedicated to Eadric. William Hurdis, who was born and died in the village but had a wider experience, was the rector in the 18th century.

Bishopstone was the home and burial place of William Catt (d 1853) the most famous of the lessees of the Tide Mills under whose proprietorship the mill complex was expanded, including a village that housed an estimated 100 people. He was undoubtedly a stern employer. Some of his working practices would be frowned upon today. He did allow men to leave the village at night to visit the pub but there was a curfew. Those he caught breaking it were confined to the village for a month.

Follow raised path to reach Yacht Club on left, the sea on right and roadway.

Having reached the coast and the English Channel at Seaford Bay the Sussex Ouse Valley Way has now been completed.

The authors do not recommend the tradition that has grown up at the end of Offa's Dyke Path of wading out to sea, minus footwear and socks, as far as is dared, but France does lie over the water...

Bishopstone Station. Turn left on road, entrance on right up steps prior to reaching railway bridge.

Car park and toilets. Continue ahead on coast road, 100m on left.

Seaford town centre and railway station. Continue ahead on coast road for another 1½ miles.

Seaford Bay

...And, quoted in many books on Sussex, Lord Tennyson writing at Blackdown in north west Sussex, the highest point in Sussex, where he spent the last years of his life, although it could be applicable to many places in Sussex.

> *"You came, and looked and loved the view*
> *Long known and loved by me,*
> *Green Sussex fading into blue,*
> *With one gray glimpse of sea."*

Further Reading

The definitive work on the Ouse and its valley is *Sussex River; Journeys along the Banks of the River Ouse* by Edna and 'Mac' McCarthy published in three slim but packed paperbacks between 1975 and 1979 but it is long out of print and access to copies is not the easiest.

A contemporary, comprehensive work lies in the future. That may tell of the success of the Sussex Ouse Restoration Trust and how it is possible to moor beside the Sloop at Freshfield or the Anchor at Barcombe and enjoy a pint before going further.

In the meantime there are many books to which reference has been made to a greater or lesser degree in the course of research and checking and cross-checking, but to flesh out the background, there are especially:

J R Armstrong, *A History of Sussex*, Phillimore 1995.

Pieter and Rita Boogaart, *A272: an Ode to a Road*, Pallas Athene 2011.

Peter Brandon, *The Kent & Sussex Weald*, Phillimore 2003.
A fitting companion volume to his earlier *The South Downs*, a classic in waiting if it has not already achieved that status. His later works on Sussex continued the tradition.

Charles Hadfield, *British Canals 8th edition*, Budding Books 1994.

Olivia Laing, *To the River*, Cannongate 2011.

Ian Nairn and Nikolas Pevsner, *The Buildings of England: Sussex*, Penguin 1965.

Leslie Oppitz, *Lost Railways of Sussex*, Countryside Books 2001.

P A L Vine, *Kent and East Sussex Waterways*, Middleton Press 1985.

Acknowledgements

The authors would like to believe that the success of the Sussex Ouse Valley Way was solely due to themselves but that would be far from the truth. The success is largely due to the good use of the support, encouragement and enthusiasm that was made available to them throughout. Creating the Way was a labour of love and it is hoped that this is communicated to all that walk it.

It is difficult to know where one should finish the list of those who should be thanked or the order in which they should be placed for there are so many that have contributed in so many ways, some of whom prefer anonymity. The authors intend to stop well short of some of the categories that have been included within Oscar acceptance speeches but there are those who cannot and must not be forgotten. The authors can only apologise to those whose contributions may have been overlooked.

Special mention has already been made by the authors of the invaluable help received from the County Councils of both East and West Sussex and the Sussex Downs Conservation Board that has now been superseded by the South Downs National Park Authority.

Invaluable encouragement was also given by both SORT (Sussex Ouse Restoration Trust) and individual members of that body. They are wished every success in their future efforts to restore the historic structures on the old Ouse Navigation.

Harveys too deserve a special mention not only for the practical sponsorship given to the project but also for consoling and supporting the authors on many an occasion before and since.

Finally mention must be made of Bridget Rose who was with the project from day one and whose design skills, ideas and advice proved invaluable to the authors.

Sussex Ouse
Restoration Trust

HARVEYS

The Circular Walks

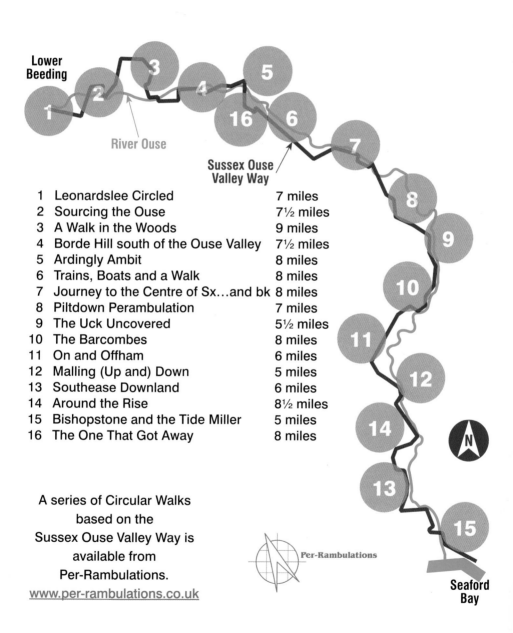

Lower Beeding

River Ouse

Sussex Ouse Valley Way

A series of Circular Walks based on the Sussex Ouse Valley Way is available from Per-Rambulations.
www.per-rambulations.co.uk

Per-Rambulations

Seaford Bay

Useful Contacts April 2012

South Downs National Park Authority **03003 031053** info@southdowns.gov.uk

East Sussex County Council **01273 481000** www.eastsussex.gov.uk

West Sussex County Council **01243 777100** www.westsussex.gov.uk

Lewes Tourist Information Centre **01273 483448** lewes.tic@lewes.gov.uk

Horsham Tourist Information Centre **01403 211661**
visitor.information@horsham.gov.uk

Seaford Tourist Information Centre **01323 897426** seaford.tic@lewes.gov.uk

National Rail Enquiries **08457 48 49 50** www.nationalrail,co.uk

Traveline (public transport) **0871 200 22 33** www.traveline.org.uk

Floodline **08459 881188** enquiries@environment-agency.gov.uk

Sussex Ouse Restoration Trust www.sxouse.org.uk

HF Holidays www.hfholidays.co.uk

Harveys Brewery, Lewes **01273 480209** www.harveys.org.uk

For up to date information concerning bed and breakfast establishments please contact the nearest Tourist Information Centre.

Some PUBS along the Way (Bed and Breakfast*)

The Crab Tree, Lower Beeding **01403 892666** www.crabtreesussex.co.uk

The Chequers*, Slaugham **01444 400239** www.the-chequers.com

The Red Lion, Handcross **01444 400292** www.redlionhandcross.co.uk

The Jolly Tanners, Staplefield **01444 400335** www.jollytanners.com

The Victory Inn, Staplefield **01444 400463** www.thevictorystaplefield.co.uk

The Bent Arms*, Lindfield **01444 483146** www.thebentarmsbandb.co.uk

The Sloop, Freshfield **01444 831219** www.thesloopinn.com

The Bull*, Newick **01825 722055** www.thebullonthegreen.co.uk

The Crown, Newick **01825 723293** www.thecrowninnnewick.co.uk

The Royal Oak*, Newick **01825 722506**
www.theroyaloakbandbandrestaurant.co.uk

The Laughing Fish, Isfield **01825 750349** www.laughingfishonline.co.uk

The Royal Oak, Barcombe **01273 400418** www.royaloakbarcombe.co.uk

The Anchor Inn, Barcombe **01273 400414** www.anchorinnandboating.co.uk

The Dorset*, Lewes **01273 474823** www.thedorsetlewes.com

The John Harvey Tavern, Lewes **01273 479880** www.johnharveytavern.co.uk

Abergavenny Arms, Rodmell **01273 472416** www.abergavennyarms.com

Back cover: looking through the Ouse Valley Viaduct